Ft. Smallwood School

Martin Luther King, Jr.

Martin Luther King, Jr.

Caroline Lazo

Peacemakers

DILLON PRESS
New York

Maxwell Macmillan Canada
Toronto

Maxwell Macmillan International
New York   Oxford   Singapore   Sydney

To Tyler

Photo Credits

Photos courtesy of AP-Wide World Photos

Book design by Carol Matsuyama

Library of Congress Cataloging-in-Publication Data

Lazo, Caroline Evensen.
    Martin Luther King, Jr. / by Caroline Lazo.
      p. cm. — (Peacemakers)
    Includes bibliographical references.
    Summary: A biography of the influential civil rights leader who won a Nobel Peace Prize for his work.
    ISBN 0-87518-618-1
    1.King, Martin Luther, Jr., 1929-1968—Juvenile literature. 2. Afro-Americans—Biography—Juvenile literature. 3. Civil rights workers—United States—Biography—Juvenile literature. 4. Baptists—United States—Clergy—Biography—Juvenile literature. [1. King, Martin Luther, Jr., 1929-1968. 2. Civil rights workers. 3. Clergy. 4. Afro-Americans—Biography.] I. Title. II. Series.
E185.97.K5L38 1994
328'.092—dc20
[B]   93-9069

Dillon Press
Macmillan Publishing Company
866 Third Avenue
New York, NY 10022

Maxwell Macmillan Canada, Inc.
1200 Eglinton Avenue East
Suite 200
Don Mills, Ontario M3C 3N1

Macmillan Publishing Company is part of the Maxwell Communication Group of Companies.

First Edition

Printed in the United States of America

10 9 8 7 6 5 4 3 2 1

Contents

Introduction

January 15 marks the birthday of Martin Luther King, Jr., the only minority person in American history to have a national holiday created in his honor. In fact only three other people have received that tribute: Christopher Columbus, George Washington, and Abraham Lincoln. And it was the "sunlight of Lincoln" that brightened the path King forged—and millions followed—to win freedom for blacks in America. But it was Mahatma Gandhi and his philosophy of nonviolence that inspired King's civil rights movement and made him the most loved (by the people) and hated (by racists) leader of his time.

When Rosa Parks, a black resident of Montgomery, Alabama, was arrested for refusing to give her seat on a bus to a white person, King began to organize nonviolent boycotts and marches on behalf of all black people who, like Rosa, were sick of being treated as slaves nearly 100 years after Lincoln had set them free. They were sick of being restricted by signs saying "Whites Only" or "No Coloreds Allowed" and sick of being unable to vote in a so-called democratic America. Above all they were sick of seeing black people lynched—hanged on trees or strung up on sign-posts—while white men laughed.

Two young marchers proudly celebrate Martin Luther King Day.   7

King, a popular Baptist preacher from Atlanta, Georgia, and his followers willingly suffered the consequences of their peaceful protests against such blatant racism in their country. Bombed, beaten, stoned, and spat upon, they continued to march for freedom and made history every mile of the way. Finally federal laws enforced equal rights for blacks in America. But laws couldn't erase the prejudice and hatred that still governed groups like the Ku Klux Klan. So King continued to educate and inspire Americans to come together—regardless of their race, color, or creed.

When discussing how he wanted to be remembered, King said:

> If you get somebody to deliver the eulogy, tell him not to talk too long. . . . Tell him not to mention I have a Nobel Peace Prize or other awards—that isn't important. I'd like somebody to say that Martin Luther King, Jr., tried to love and serve humanity . . . and to leave a committed life behind. . . . If you want to, say that I was a drum major. Say that I was a drum major for justice. Say that I was a drum major for peace.

The tomb of Martin Luther King, Jr.

After King's shocking assassination on April 4, 1968, somebody did say that—and much more. "No words of mine can fill the void of the eloquent voice that has been stilled," President Lyndon B. Johnson said. "But this I do believe deeply: The dream of Dr. Martin Luther King has not died with him. . . . The forces of divisiveness know that America shall not be ruled by the bullet, but only by the ballot."

Pope Paul VI told the world that the killing of Martin Luther King "weighed on the conscience of all mankind." And King's friend, the Reverend Jesse Jackson, said, "He didn't just talk brotherhood; he was a brother. He didn't just talk friendship; he was a friend. He didn't just wish for change; he changed things."

Martin Luther King organized many demonstrations in his fight for peace, including protests against the war in Vietnam.

"Separate but Equal"

After Abraham Lincoln issued the Emancipation Proclamation in 1863, slaves in the southern states were legally free. The Thirteenth Amendment to the Constitution, ratified in 1865, officially ended slavery throughout the United States. Plantation owners whose slaves had come from Africa in chains to work for them were forced to let them go. But to the uneducated and illiterate blacks (called Negroes then) freedom was both wonderful and frightening. Where could they go? What could they do? Other than slave labor, what were they *qualified* to do?

The South suffered great destruction during the Civil War, and even white people had to struggle to rebuild their lives. To the whites the blacks were outcasts, nobodies. Federal troops, assigned to enforce the Emancipation Proclamation, protected the blacks in the hostile, postwar environment. But at the end of Reconstruction (1865-1877) those forces disbanded, and southern whites, still angered at their defeat by the North made new laws of their own. The decision in the case of *Plessy v. Ferguson* (1896), upheld by the Supreme Court, ensured continued superiority of whites and gave segregation a foothold in the South that lasted for 58 years. It ruled that as long as facilities for blacks were equal to those for whites, segregation by race was constitutional. The ruling was known as the "separate but equal" law, but in practice only the "separate" part was enforced; facilities for blacks were never equal to those for the whites.

While whites used front entrances to buildings, blacks had to use back or side doors. Public parks, as well as hotels, motels, and restaurants, refused to allow blacks inside at all, and black children could visit the zoo only after the white people had left. "Blacks were forced to take the freight elevator in department stores," biographer Nancy Shuker wrote. "A Negro or 'colored person'—as black people were referred to then—might be served a soda or ice cream from a window at the side of the store. For blacks, the treat would always be in a paper cup." The glassware was reserved for white customers only.

These laws, as practiced in the South, were called Jim Crow laws, after a white clownlike character who blackened his face to imitate Negroes and make white audiences laugh.

Even the hospitals were segregated. When famous blues singer Bessie Smith was injured in an automobile accident, she was rushed to one hospital after another. None of them would admit her, and she died. Famous or unknown, it made no difference in the early to mid-1900s in America's deep South. If you were black, you were nobody.

Following the Civil War, many former slaves fled north—never realizing they would awaken demons of prejudice lying dormant there for centuries. "The strait-jackets of race prejudice and discrimination do not wear only Southern labels," Martin Luther King, Jr., wrote years later. "The subtle, psychological technique of the North has approached in its ugliness and victimization of the Negro the outright terror and open brutality of the South."

By 1955, at the age of 26, King was ready to confront those demons that had haunted the history of black people in America. He was ready to avenge—non-violently—the slurs against his father and mother, the attacks against the poor blacks throughout Atlanta, and the inferior education of black children everywhere. "Being a Negro in America is not a comfortable existence," he said. "It means the pain of watching your children grow up with clouds of inferiority in their mental skies. It means having your legs cut off, and then being condemned for being a cripple."

As the son of a respected Baptist minister, King suffered less than most black children who grew up in the South. His parents did everything possible to protect their children from the humiliation of discrimination, but they could not escape the awful reality of racism surrounding them. Riding home on a bus one day, young King and his teacher had to give up their seats to two white men, and King would never forget the experience. The ride home was long and tiring, standing up all the way. And he had just won an award for his speech entitled "The Negro and the Constitution." What happened, he wondered, to the basic, constitutional rights to life, liberty, and the pursuit of happiness? And "justice for all"?

Bright, curious, and caring, young King began to question the separate-but-equal law of the land. Watching his parents stand up to the demons of prejudice did more to influence his future involvement in the fight for civil rights than anything else. He could remember, for example, the day he was riding with his father, who accidentally drove through a stop sign:

Reverend King during the 1956 trials over the Montgomery, Alabama, bus boycott

A policeman pulled up to the car and said, "All right, boy, pull over and let me see your license." My father replied indignantly, "I'm no boy." Then, pointing to me, "This is a boy. I am a man, and until you call me one, I will not listen to you." The policeman was so shocked that he wrote the ticket up nervously and left the scene as quickly as possible.

With this heritage, it is not surprising that I had . . . learned to abhor segregation.

King was only a small boy when he heard the policeman insult his father, and was just a teenager when he and his teacher boarded that bus and had to give up their seats so two white people could sit down. "The stuff of nightmares," he once called such episodes. But years later he would turn those nightmares into a dream—a dream that one day he would live in a nation where his children—and all children—"will not be judged by the color of their skin, but by the content of their character. . . where little black boys and black girls will be able to join hands with little white boys and white girls and walk together as sisters and brothers."

Strengthened by loving parents, family, and friends, King was determined to turn his dream into reality, and like Gandhi, to endure the suffering along the way.

Living Up to a Legend

Perhaps the first challenge facing Martin Luther King, Jr., was his name—Martin Luther. Luther was the famous German monk who, in 1529, rebelled against the Church of Rome and began the Protestant Reformation. Brave, bold, and visionary, Martin Luther's image was not easy to live up to, not an easy name to bear. Luther was well-known for his writings, including this famous psalm and hymn:

> A mighty fortress is our God,
> A bulwark never failing;
> Our helper He amid the flood
> Of mortal ills prevailing.

But Luther's methods of attracting followers to his faith clouded the beauty of his hymns. Jews, for example, who refused to convert to his new Protestant religion were sent to "work camps" and kept there until they converted. He hoped to see Germany "purified"—with everyone Christian, everyone Protestant. No freedom. No choice. Centuries later, Adolf Hitler would cite Luther's work-camp idea to justify his own purification plan to send Jews

and other minority groups to concentration camps—not to convert them, but to kill them.

That memory of Martin Luther would be a burden for his namesake, Martin Luther King, Jr. But King would work hard to make his own name, and by doing so would give the name Martin Luther new meaning, new glory. In seeking civil rights for blacks, King would bring attention to the injustices experienced by all minorities. "When we let freedom ring," he said, "we will be able to speed up that day when all of God's children, black men and white men, Jews and Gentiles, Protestants and Catholics, will be able to join hands and sing in the words of that old Negro spiritual, 'Free at last! Free at last! Thank God almighty, we are free at last!'"

Martin Luther King, Jr., was born on January 15, 1929, in Atlanta, Georgia. At first he was called Michael—after his father—but a few years later his father (known as Daddy King) changed both his and his son's names to Martin Luther. Young Martin was nicknamed M.L. He was a middle child, born between his older sister Christine and his younger brother Alfred Daniel ("A.D.")

In 1932, during the Great Depression, Daddy King

Martin Luther King, Jr., contemplates his
speech before a news conference.

became pastor of Ebenezer Baptist Church in Atlanta. Though the Depression caused the majority of blacks to depend on government assistance, Pastor King's church prospered, and the congregation tripled in size. He and his wife, Alberta, were able to live in a quiet, middle-class neighborhood where they hoped to shelter their three children from the racism rampant in Atlanta and throughout the South, the racism that had haunted Daddy King all his life. Unlike Alberta, he had received little protection from prejudice while growing up in Georgia.

Daddy King was the son of a sharecropper and had no formal education. He took high-school courses at night, and through careful study of the Bible, taught himself to be a preacher. He grew up hearing the word *nigger* routinely, and he prayed that someday people would erase that word—and all derogatory names directed toward blacks—from their vocabulary. Alberta's father was the beloved pastor of the Ebenezer Baptist Church prior to Daddy King, and he was the first president of Atlanta's chapter of the National Association for the Advancement of Colored People (NAACP). Because of his efforts to end Georgia's racist laws and to build a school for black

Ebenezer Baptist Church, where Martin Luther King, Sr., and Martin Luther King, Jr., were co-pastors

children in Atlanta, he was given an honorary Ph.D. from Morehouse College. He was happy that he could give his daughter Alberta a good education. She studied music at Spelman College in Atlanta.

When Alberta's father died, Daddy King took over as pastor. He and Alberta shared their house with her mother, who became known, affectionately, as Mama to all three King children—Christine, Martin, and Alfred. Anxious to continue his education, Daddy King earned his bachelor's degree in divinity from Morehouse College and pursued a Ph.D. at Morris Brown College. But he still found time to work hard for equal rights for blacks. Following in his father-in-law's footsteps, Daddy King not only gave inspiring sermons but also became active in the NAACP, and though unsuccessful, organized a protest march to win blacks' right to vote.

The church was the core of the Kings' family life. It unified and inspired them. Though young Martin was no angel as a child, he loved to memorize hymns, and while only in kindergarten, he could recite entire chapters from the Bible. He and his brother battled with each other just as other siblings did, but his wildest behavior usually resulted from feelings of guilt. Once the boys slid down the banister and bumped into their grandmother at the bottom, knocking her down. Martin was sure she had died from the fall, so he ran upstairs and jumped out a window!

Years later, while Martin was watching a parade instead of studying, Mama suffered a heart attack and died. Once again, he was filled with guilt, but his father helped him to deal with his grief and erase his guilt. He told

Reverend King preaches to an eager congregation.

Martin that it was God's decision to "call her back to Him." Later, Martin recalled that Gandhi, too, had suffered deep feelings of guilt when his own father died. Both men learned an early lesson about death being a part of life. As a result their fear of death was replaced with a peace of mind that helped them face life's challenges with great courage later on.

Ft. Smallwood School

A Taste of Freedom

No matter how hard Martin's parents tried to shelter him from racism they knew such protection couldn't last forever. Even as a young boy Martin showed unusual sensitivity to the feelings of others, and was an extremely smart student. He had many friends, and one of them happened to be white. However, before entering first grade, the boy told Martin that their friendship had to end, because Martin was black. Because of segregated schools, the boys would have been separated in any case. But even though other children had learned to accept segregation laws, Martin could not. He had lost a friend—not because of illness or death, but because of his color! He couldn't understand it, and he bombarded his parents with questions: Why can't children of different colors go to school together? Why aren't we all treated the same? Who made the segregation laws, and why?

Martin's parents never failed to answer Martin's questions. They told him about his African ancestors and the torture they endured in America. And though Lincoln had freed the slaves, racism was still alive in Atlanta and throughout the South. In spite of "Whites Only" signs everywhere, Martin's mother tried to convince her son that he was somebody; and she told him that if he had faith in himself, someday he might overcome the racial prejudice that surrounded him. She assured him that when he was older he would have a better understanding of the causes of injustice, and, maybe, like his father and grandfather, he might work to end it.

When Martin became a teenager he realized that in order to influence others he would have to learn to speak well in public and become not just a bright student, but a respected one. And he did. After skipping several grades, Martin entered Booker T. Washington High School and finished at the age of 15. After graduation he entered a public-speaking contest that tested his knowledge of English and history as well as his speaking ability. Though he won a prize, his joy turned quickly to sadness and anger when he had to give up his seat to a white person on that long, memorable bus ride home. The ride would be a turning point in his life. When he decided to enroll in Morehouse College at the age of 15, he was ready to question what the church was doing to rid the state of racial inequality. This meant he had to challenge his own father's role as a Baptist minister. If blacks take the Bible seriously, he wondered, how could they remain submissive to whites? Must blacks have to wait to go to heaven to find equal justice? These were just a few of the questions on Martin's mind in 1944 when he filled out the application to Morehouse, an all-black college in Atlanta. He was immediately accepted.

Before the fall semester began, Martin joined a Morehouse summer-jobs program, which gave him a chance to go north and work on a tobacco farm in Connecticut. But, more important, it gave him his first real chance to experience freedom in America. In Connecticut he could use front entrances to theaters; he could sit next to whites; he could eat in the restaurant of his choice. He was overwhelmed with joy! But the summer ended quickly and his happiness was short-lived, as biographer Nancy Shuker recounts:

> The train trip back to Atlanta returned M.L. to the reality of life in the South. As the train entered Virginia he went to the dining car to have his supper. He was shown to a table in a far corner, where a curtain was drawn around him so that

A young Martin Luther King, Jr., listens to a speaker during an assembly at Morehouse College.

other passengers would not have to watch a black man eat.

When Martin entered Morehouse, he was unsure of the course his career should take. His father had expected him to follow in his footsteps and become a Baptist minister. But the law attracted Martin, because he realized laws would have to be changed to win freedom for blacks. Could the church help to accomplish that goal? So far, he knew it had not.

Through the guidance of Dr. Benjamin Mays, the president of Morehouse, Martin discovered that, indeed, the church could move blacks in ways laws could not. It could awaken them to their God-given power to seek truth and justice through faith. But, Martin said later, "We must learn that to expect God to do everything while we do nothing is not faith but superstition."

The stocky, 5'8"-tall student with the rich, resonant speaking voice became one of Morehouse's most popular young men on campus. Already nicknamed Tweed because of his love of good-looking sport jackets, Martin was noticed for his style as well as his outgoing personality. He seemed to always remember his mother's words—that even though he was black in the white-ruled South, he was somebody. His confidence was contagious; people felt good just being around him. Sparks of the charisma that would later attract world attention were already catching fire in college. Young women at Morehouse felt honored to receive a poem or letter from him, and his male friends loved to join him in card games.

Though some have said that Martin seemed to lack humor, those who knew him well said just the opposite. His imitations of wild, evangelistic preachers, for example, made everyone laugh. And the athletic-looking King studied the violin and developed a lifelong love of music; classical as well as jazz.

During his senior year at Morehouse College, at the age of 17, Martin made his decision to become a minister. His proud father gave him a chance to deliver a guest sermon at the Ebenezer Baptist Church. Huge crowds came to hear him, and for weeks people talked about the young pastor with the "stirring voice." Though he didn't know it at the time, Martin Luther King, Jr., was already on his way to winning worldwide acclaim.

New Lessons from Old Leaders

Strengthened by Dr. Mays's belief that churches could help blacks pursue their civil rights, and encouraged by his father's faith in him as a preacher, Martin entered Crozer Seminary in Chester, Pennsylvania, to earn his divinity degree. In that same year, 1947, as Martin was beginning his life work to secure civil rights for blacks, Mahatma Gandhi was ending his long struggle to win peace and equal justice for his people in India. After years of nonviolent protests, strikes, and boycotts, Gandhi and his followers finally won India's freedom from the British Empire. Could nonviolent protest succeed in America's racist South? Could it bring freedom at last for blacks? King was anxious to learn more about Gandhi's philosophy and the possibility of putting it into action in America. Later, after a thorough study of *satyagraha* (active but nonviolent resistance to injustice), King wrote:

> Gandhi was probably the first person in history to lift the love ethic of Jesus above mere interaction between individuals to a powerful and effective social force on a large scale. . . . It

was in this Gandhian emphasis on love and non-violence that I discovered the method for social reform that I had been seeking for so many months.

When he graduated from Crozer, Martin enrolled in Boston University to earn a Ph.D. While there he met and fell in love with Coretta Scott, a student at the New England Conservatory of Music. She had planned on a career in music, and marriage—especially to a preacher—was the last thing on her mind! "I thought I did not want to marry a minister," Coretta wrote, "but Martin was an unusual person . . . such a good man. If he ever did something a little wrong, or committed a selfish act, his conscience devoured him. At the same time, he was so alive and fun to be with. He had a strength that he imparted to me and others he met."

In 1953 Martin and Coretta were married. The following year they moved to Montgomery, Alabama, where Martin became pastor of the Dexter Avenue Church. Returning to the South was a shock after so many months of freedom up north. Even though in 1954 the U.S. Supreme Court ruled that segregated schools were

Coretta Scott King greets Martin after an appearance in court.

unconstitutional, southern whites reacted violently to the ruling and seemed even more determined to keep blacks "in their place." Ku Klux Klan members started fires all over Alabama. Crosses went up in flames. High poll taxes at election places made it impossible for most blacks to vote. Old Jim Crow laws still governed the South, and nothing seemed to change.

Public transportation—and all public facilities—remained segregated. Though blacks paid their bus fares at the front of the bus, they had to leave the bus and walk to the rear door to enter and sit down. The front section was reserved for whites only—just as it had been when Martin was a boy. But on December 1, 1955, Rosa Parks, a black seamstress in a local department store, boarded a bus in Montgomery, and her ride home that day made history.

Tired after a hard day at work, Rosa politely refused to obey the bus driver's order to give up her seat to a white man. The driver left the bus to find a policeman, and Rosa was arrested. She called a friend, E. D. Nixon, who posted bail for her and later called Martin and Coretta to tell them what had happened. A boycott of the Montgomery bus system, he told them, was the only way "to show we will not take this sort of thing any longer."

The incident was just the kind of opportunity King needed to test the theory of nonviolent protest. If blacks stopped riding buses, the city would lose money, and the nation would soon hear about their bold but

Dr. King and Dr. Abernathy hold a conference to announce their plans for fighting segregation.

peaceful action. So King called a meeting of black leaders, including E. D. Nixon and Martin's friend and fellow pastor, Ralph Abernathy, to discuss their plan for non-cooperation with segregated buses in Montgomery. King and the others met at the Dexter Avenue Church where they organized the Montgomery Improvement Association and elected King as their president. They scheduled their first boycott for December 5, four days after Rosa was arrested.

Empty buses filled the streets of the city, as more and more blacks refused to ride them. The boycott was a huge success. In the following year more than 50,000 black people stopped riding the buses. They walked, sometimes many miles, to work; black cab drivers drove as many as possible for only 10 cents a ride; many rode in car pools. The entire Montgomery bus system was nearly brought to a halt. Nonviolent protest worked! As the bus system continued to lose money, city officials began a campaign to arrest blacks for any reason they could think of. Martin himself was jailed for driving 30 miles per hour in a 25-mile-per-hour zone. But when huge crowds of blacks responded to King's arrest by quietly surrounding the jail, he was

Reverend Ralph Abernathy, Martin Luther King, Jr., Reverend Glenn Smiley, and an unidentified woman ride the first nonsegregated bus in Montgomery, Alabama.

released. King had given blacks a new self-confidence never felt before—a certain "strength," as Coretta called it.

Arrests were followed by death threats to blacks. Once, while Martin was at a rally, Coretta and their first child, two-month-old Yolanda, were at home with a friend. Suddenly, in the quiet of the night, a bomb was thrown on the front porch and exploded. No one was hurt, but the incident at once enraged and saddened Martin and his followers. They knew they would have to work much harder to break down racial barriers. At the same time, their nonviolent action against the bus system was front-page news across the country, and their bold but peaceful protest resulted in a new ruling by the Supreme Court. Alabama's practice of segregation on city buses violated the Constitution, and, therefore, had to be abolished.

On December 21, 1956, King, Abernathy, and a white minister rode the first nonsegregated bus in Montgomery; they sat together in the front seats, and once again, a bus ride made history. Gandhi's prophecy, stated in 1935, seemed to be coming true. "It may be," Gandhi said, "that through the American Negro the unadulterated message of nonviolence will be delivered to the world."

Off and Running

By 1957 King had become a national figure. In little more than a year, *Time* magazine reported, he had "risen from nowhere to become one of the nation's remarkable leaders." Like a champion race horse, King was off and running—and determined not to stop until blacks had won the same rights white people had enjoyed for centuries. Cheered on by blacks throughout the city, King had burst open the gates of Montgomery and was already on his way to more boycotts—in Mobile, Birmingham, and Tallahassee. Various black groups banded together to form the Southern Christian Leadership Conference (SCLC), and they elected Martin their president. He received invitations to speak all over the world, and in 1959, with Coretta by his side, he visited India and the shrine of Mahatma Gandhi in New Delhi. "I am a disciple of Gandhi," he always said.

King was torn between his desire to spend more time with his children, Yolanda, Martin, Dexter, and Bernice, and his total commitment to the civil rights movement. He knew the only way to provide a decent future for his children was to work full time to knock down the roadblocks of racism, and he hoped the children would

Martin Luther and Coretta Scott King with three of their children—Martin, Dexter, and Yolanda.

understand. According to Yolanda, now a grown woman, they did. They adored their father. "We played a lot," she told *Life* magazine. "We played ball in the house and my mother would come in and say, 'Martin, Martin, you're going to break something.' And he'd say, 'Okay, okay, Corrie'—and she'd leave, and we'd go right back. . . . My memories are full of laughter. I just remember laughing, laughing."

In 1960 Martin and Coretta moved back to Atlanta, where Martin joined his father as co-pastor of the Ebenezer Baptist Church. By 1961 masses of whites had joined King's movement, and the Congress of Racial Equality organized the Freedom Riders to test the Supreme Court ruling to integrate buses. They rode from Washington, D.C. to New Orleans, and were beaten, bombed, and stabbed by white mobs who met the buses at stops along the way. Some of the riders were imprisoned for causing the trouble, which, of course, they did not. Undaunted, the Freedom Riders kept going. And whole black families marched together to protest racial discrimination in department stores and restaurants, too.

Sit-ins were staged in restaurants to call attention to

Martin Luther King, Jr., leads a group of Freedom Riders on a march.

the blatant segregation there. Only 18 years old at
the time, black Congressman John Lewis from Georgia
would never forget the white men who kicked him as he

walked in and sat down, and who put cigarettes out in a woman's hair.

Fortunately there were moments of comic relief to remember as well. Once, during a sit-in, a young boy asked his mother, "Is this what we've been marching for—to eat here?"

"Yes," she said, "and to feel free to eat in any restaurant of our choice, just as white people do. By daring to sit here until we're served, we prove how much we care about that freedom . . ."

"Well, it's not worth it," the boy interrupted. "The french fries are awful!"

Many blacks wondered why President John F. Kennedy didn't pay more attention to the struggle of the blacks to gain equal rights. Why didn't his administration push for federal civil rights legislation? One reason was that in the early 1960s Kennedy and Congress were preoccupied with communism in Cuba and the buildup of missiles there—just 20 minutes by plane from Key West, Florida. Also, FBI Director J. Edgar Hoover, often called a closet racist, disliked Martin, and he criticized the civil rights movement. More than 30 years later Americans learned that Hoover used illegal tactics to spy on King, and that his criticism of King was totally unjustified. Many believed that Hoover was jealous of King's increasing power—a power based on love and reason, not fear and deceit.

But Hoover was just one of King's enemies. In addition, there was the ever-present, tyrannical Ku Klux Klan; Alabama's governor, George Wallace; and Birmingham's Public Safety Director, Eugene "Bull" Connor, among others. Though Wallace later changed his attitude, while he was governor he promised "Segregation now, segregation tomorrow, segregation forever!" And Bull Connor commanded his men to use police dogs, fire hoses, and clubs to beat back the blacks when they marched peacefully through his city in 1963. Connor got a court injunction against the demonstrators, and King and other leaders were arrested. While in jail, King wrote his famous "Letter from Birmingham Jail" to some white ministers who had criticized his protesting in Birmingham. He wrote:

I am in Birmingham because injustice is here. . . . It is unfortunate that demonstrations are taking place in Birmingham, but it is even more unfortunate that the city's white power structure left the Negro community with no alternative. . . . We have waited for more than 340 years for our constitutional and God-given rights. . . . Perhaps it is easy for those who have never felt the stinging darts of segregation to say, "Wait." But when you have seen vicious mobs lynch your mothers and fathers at will and drown your sisters and brothers at whim; when you see the hate-filled policemen curse, kick, and even kill your black brothers and sisters; when . . . you take a cross-country drive and find it necessary to sleep night after night in the uncomfortable corners of your automobile because no motel will accept you; when . . . you are forever fighting a degenerating sense of "nobodiness"—then you will understand why we find it difficult to wait. . . . I hope, sirs, you can understand our legitimate and unavoidable impatience.

Bull Connor seemed to be unaware that when his bloodthirsty police dogs attacked blacks in Birmingham,

Photos like this one depicting police attacks on black protestors helped awaken the nation to the civil rights movement.

photographs of brutality were taken and flashed around the world. One photo, in particular, stunned President Kennedy and alarmed reasonable people everywhere. Such publicity awakened America to the widespread bigotry in the nation, and prompted federal focus on civil rights legislation. On May 20, 1963, the U.S. Supreme Court ruled that Birmingham's segregation laws were unconstitutional.

But Alabama's governor, George Wallace, remained as racist as ever. He stood at the front door of the University of Alabama to personally prevent two black students from entering. Even though one student, James Meredith, had previously enrolled in the University of Mississippi by a Supreme Court order, and had been escorted on campus by U.S. marshals, Wallace did his best to block such integration in his state. He failed, because President Kennedy sent the National Guard to the scene and told Wallace to step aside. The next day, prominent NAACP leader Medgar Evers was assassinated in Mississippi. Racism was still alive in the South, but Americans from New York to California were enraged and ready to join King's march to the Lincoln Memorial in Washington, D.C. on August 28, 1963. "That day," one marcher said, "we heard the speech of a lifetime."

Half a million people stretched from the steps of the Lincoln Memorial to the Washington Monument

Martin Luther King, Jr., addresses a crowd of thousands outside the Lincoln Memorial.

to listen to King talk about his dream:

> I have a dream that one day this nation will rise up and live out the true meaning of its creed: "We hold these truths to be self-evident; that all men are created equal."
>
> I have a dream that one day on the red hills of Georgia the sons of former slaves and the sons of former slaveowners will be able to sit down together at the table of brotherhood. . . .
>
> I have a dream that my four little children will one day live in a nation where they will not be judged by the color of their skin but by the content of their character.
>
> I have a dream today . . .

After the rally King and other civil rights leaders were greeted by President Kennedy at the White House. Just three months later President Kennedy was killed, and the whole world mourned the loss of the young president who had shown so much promise and had given hope to so many people.

Fulfilling the Dream

When President Lyndon B. Johnson moved into the White House, passage of Kennedy's civil rights legislation was his number-one priority. He consulted with King, and they became friends. But in spite of King's immense popularity, some—even his fellow blacks—opposed his philosophy of nonviolence, even though they respected him as a great leader. Malcolm X, the Black Muslim leader, and Stokely Carmichael, leader of the Student Nonviolent Coordination Committee (SNCC) believed in "Black Power" and more revolutionary ways to win power if nonviolence failed. The majority, however, not only respected King but idolized him, and even saw in him a messiah. When he wasn't marching or being sent to jail, he was meeting with world leaders, including India's Prime Minister Nehru and Pope Paul VI. He was *Time* magazine's Man of the Year in 1964. But 1964 also marked the beginning of nationwide riots—from New York to Los Angeles—as whites fought against voting rights for blacks and desegregation of public places, and blacks struggled for equal justice.

King refused to participate in any violent protest, and continued to teach nonviolence. In July 1964, the Civil

Rights Act became law, but it overlooked voting rights and housing for the poor. And white racists did their best to keep it that way—especially in the South. In Mississippi, for example, blacks were bombed in their homes and even at church, and they were beaten in the streets, and jailed. But Martin never let go of his dream, and stepped up his marches for voting rights. In spite of white fanaticism, King continued to speak out, and the world watched and listened.

In December 1964, King was awarded the Nobel Peace Prize for his efforts to obtain peace and justice for blacks in the United States. Coretta, Martin's brother A.D. (also a minister), and Ralph Abernathy traveled to Oslo, Norway, where he accepted the world's most respected prize for peace.

I am mindful, that in Birmingham, Alabama, our children, crying out for brotherhood, were answered with fire hoses, snarling dogs, and even death. I am mindful that in Mississippi young people seeking to secure the right to vote were brutalized and murdered. Therefore I must ask

why this prize is awarded to a movement...which has not won the very peace and brotherhood which is the essence of the Nobel Prize. After contemplation I conclude that this award...is a profound recognition that nonviolence is the answer to the crucial political and racial questions of our time—the need for man to overcome oppression without resorting to violence.

The prize added new momentum to King's civil rights movement, and the next few years brought great victories for blacks, and great sacrifices, too. "Freedom," King said, "has always been an expensive thing. History is fit testimony to the fact that freedom is rarely gained without sacrifice and self-denial."

On February 21, 1965, Malcolm X was murdered by blacks in New York City. A few weeks later demonstrators were beaten back on their way from Selma to Montgomery, Alabama. They were marching to protest the poll tax, intelligence tests, and other measures that prevented blacks from voting. But on March 21 federal troops were sent to Selma to protect the demonstrators en route.

Dr. King displays his Nobel Prize medal.

"Walk together, children, don't get weary," King told them, "and it will lead us to the promised land. And Alabama will be a new Alabama, and America will be a new America."

King led more than 3,000 marchers out of Selma that day, and by the time they reached Montgomery more than 25,000 had joined them. With Ralph Abernathy on one side of him, and Ralph Bunche, a founder of the United Nations, and Rabbi Abraham Heschel on the other, King had marched to another victory for nonviolent protest. The national Voting Rights Act became law on August 6, 1965. And King's friend and ally Attorney General Robert Kennedy helped to explain and enforce the law throughout the nation.

When urging Congress to pass the Voting Rights Act, President Johnson used the slogan of the civil rights movement, "We Shall Overcome." Seven months later, he repeated it—along with thousands of others—when the Supreme Court of the United States ruled that all poll taxes were unconstitutional.

The following year Martin widened his crusade for peace and justice to include speeches against the Vietnam War. And he continued to lead marches to help bring about desegregation of schools. On March 12, 1967, all of Alabama's public schools were officially ordered to de-segregate. That same year Martin wrote his last book *The Trumpet of Conscience*, which was preceded by *Stride Toward Freedom*, *Strength to Love*, *Why We Can't Wait*, and *Where Do We Go From Here?* Sporadic rioting continued throughout the country, and black leaders A. Philip Randolf, Roy Wilkins, and Whitney Young joined King in pleading for an end to rioting in America. Riots, King said, "proved ineffective and damaging to the civil rights cause and the entire nation."

While planning a poor people's march on Washington—a march that would combine blacks, American Indians, Hispanics, and poor whites from Appalachia—King received a call from a fellow pastor who asked for his help in Memphis. Black sanitation workers had suffered long enough from low wages and other unlawful discrimination, he said. So in spite of the city's efforts to stop him, King led thousands of demonstrators through downtown Memphis to show support for the striking workers.

A few days later, as the strike continued, King gave his

Martin Luther King greets supporters during a tour to encourage blacks to vote.

prophetic "mountain top" speech—often called one of the most moving speeches in American history:

> If I lived in China . . . maybe I could understand the denial of certain basic First Amendment privileges, because they hadn't committed themselves to that over there. But somewhere I read of the freedom of assembly. Somewhere I read of the freedom of speech. Somewhere I read of the freedom of the press. Somewhere I read that the greatness of America is the right to protest for right. And so, just as I say, we aren't going to let any injunction turn us around. We are going on. . . . We've got some difficult days ahead. But it doesn't matter with me now, because I've been to the mountain top. And I don't mind. Like anybody, I would like to live a long life; longevity has its place. But I'm not concerned about that now. I just want to do God's will. And He's allowed me to go up to the mountain. I've looked over. And I've *seen* the promised land. I may not get there with you. But I want you to know tonight that we

as a people will get to the promised land. And I'm happy tonight, I'm not worried about anything. I'm not fearing any man. Mine eyes have seen the glory of the coming of the Lord.

The next day, on April 4, 1968, King stood on the balcony of Memphis's Lorraine Motel and talked with friends Jesse Jackson and Ben Branch. Suddenly a shot was heard: a rifle shot. It struck King, and he clutched his neck and collapsed. He died in St. Joseph's Hospital in Memphis, and once again America went into mourning.

James Earl Ray, a white man, was convicted of the crime, but years later people questioned his role as the mastermind of the murder. New evidence suggested a conspiracy—a conspiracy that perhaps involved King's old enemy, J. Edgar Hoover. To date, the questions remain unanswered and Ray remains in prison.

On April 9, 1968, five days after the assassination, more than 800 people filled the Ebenezer Baptist Church in Atlanta for King's memorial service. Outside an estimated 100,000 people heard the service over loudspeakers. The crowd stood quietly as the Reverend Ralph

Mourners throng around King's casket as it is carried into Ebenezer Baptist Church.

Abernathy and others said prayers and words of praise for the leader they adored.

They said he was a drum major for justice. They said he was a drum major for peace. They said that Martin Luther King, Jr., loved and served humanity. . . and left a committed life behind.

For Further Reading

King, Coretta Scott. *My Life with Martin Luther King, Jr.* New York: Holt, Rinehart & Winston, 1969.

King, Martin Luther, Jr. *The Trumpet of Conscience.* New York: Harper & Row, 1968.

_____. *Why We Can't Wait.* New York: Penguin Books, 1964.

Oates, Stephen B. *Let the Trumpet Sound: The Life of Martin Luther King, Jr.* New York: Harper & Row, 1982.

Quayle, Louise. *Martin Luther King, Jr.: Dreams For A Nation.* New York: Fawcett Columbine, 1989.

Shuker, Nancy. *Martin Luther King.* New York: Chelsea House, 1985.

Index

About the Author

Caroline Evensen Lazo was born in Minneapolis, Minnesota. She spent much of her childhood visiting museums and attending plays written by her mother, Isobel Evensen, whose work earned national acclaim and became a lasting source of inspiration for her daughter.

Ms. Lazo attended the University of Oslo, Norway, and received a B.A. in Art History from the University of Minnesota. She has written extensively about art and architecture, and is the author of many books for young people, including *The Terra Cotta Army of Emperor Qin*, *Missing Treasure*, and *Endangered Species*.